Bundle o' Tinder

For Aunt Ann
with love from
Rose Kelleher

Bundle o' Tinder

Rose Kelleher

WAYWISER

First published in 2008 by

THE WAYWISER PRESS

14 Lyncroft Gardens, Ewell, Surrey KT17 1UR, UK
P.O. Box 6205, Baltimore, MD 21206, USA
www.waywiser-press.com

Managing Editor
Philip Hoy

Associate Editors
Joseph Harrison   Clive Watkins   Greg Williamson

A CIP catalogue record for this book is available from the British Library

ISBN 978-1-904130-33-8

Printed and bound by
Cromwell Press Ltd., Trowbridge, Wiltshire

Acknowledgements

Thanks to the editors of the following publications, in which some of these poems first appeared: *Anon*: "Asperger's Muse," "Ditty," "Guadalupe," "Hologram," "Impulse," "Parking Garage," "The Rectangle"; *Atlanta Review*: "Poor Dolores"; *The Barefoot Muse*: "Lye"; *The Chimaera*: "Scrape," "The Petition," "To My Husband, Poetry,"; *The Dark Horse*: "Neanderthal Flute Song," "Not Our Dog"; *The Eleventh Muse*: "Rays at Cape Hatteras"; *First Things*: "Flipside"; *iota*: "The Poet Who Will Win This Competition"; *Lucid Rhythms*: "Noted Sadomasochists," "Penal Rosary," "Zeitoun"; Measure: "Lourdes"; *The Shit Creek Review*: "Brockton Man," "Doré's Engravings," "Laissez-faire," "Love Sonnet," "Mortimer," "Sea Monster," "Shotgun"; *Snakeskin*: "Gingernut," "Lovesick," "Random Sextet"; *Snow Monkey*: "Business Trip"; *Umbrella*: "Famine Ship," "The Hybrid," "Old School"; *Worm*: "The Pig and the Pearl," "War of the Worlds"; *Znine*: "Made in Minnesota."

Special thanks to my friends at Eratosphere who have been so generous with their advice and support.

Contents

God

Science

People

Contents

Contents

Foreword by Richard Wilbur

Rose Kelleher's poems are everywhere the work of a sharp intelligence, a good heart, and a great technical gift, and yet there is such variety in this first book that it would be hard to single out some one poem as representative. Perhaps it might be the very first, "Asperger's Muse," which in hypnotic lines tells something of the motive for worship. Or it might be a little poem like "Lye," in which off-rhyme artfully reflects the scuffed textures of New England. Or it might be the wonderful sonnet "The First Uprising," which intertwines the Eden story with that of our evolution into erect creatures, devoting the octave to that development and the sestet to its consequences. It might be the virtuoso sequence "At Sea," in which various human behaviours are given marine metaphors, and in which the section called "Breakers" is full of jarring knowledge of human heartlessness.

I suspend my list of good poems, lest it go on and on. *Bundle o' Tinder* is a thoughtful book, divided into thematic sections, a book of wide reference and observation. It is very unlike the claustrally personal work of which one sees too much at present; at the same time, it is strongly personal, in the sense that its tone and vision are distinctive and recognizable. This is that rare thing, a first book in which the poet's voice has been fully found.

I am grateful to Rose Kelleher for providing me, as final judge of the Anthony Hecht Poetry Prize, with a chance to be judicious. And it makes me happy to think how much Anthony Hecht would have relished her work.

Cummington, Massachussetts,
June 2008

God

Asperger's Muse

Once again he's chanting in
a metronomic monotone
the numbers that he's memorized
without a pause for inhalation,
back and forth, a reassuring
rhythm. He has sung his favorite
song so often I should know it:
3.141592
65358979
32384626;
that's as much as I remember.
He, however, keeps on going,
eyes averted, elbows held
as if by magnets to his ribs.
He does it when he's nervous. If
you try to interrupt him, that
will only make him sing it louder.
43383279
50288419
71693993;
Seeking spoken sanctuary
in the perfect circle's key,
he draws a closed perimeter
around himself; and though I cannot
understand the tongue he speaks,
I know he sings a hymn to something
steady, central, infinite.

The Rectangle

A jungle gym, a see-saw, and a patch
of sand have snipped a corner from St. Paul's
parking lot. The wheelchair ramp is new;
phlox now crowds the walk. Behind a yawn
of double doors, the floors are fresh-swept green;

thrown out, the squares of burgundy and tan
scuffed up by hundreds of schoolchildren's shoes
in lines of two. In this fluorescent light,
the Virgin Mary with her chipped half-smile
looks out of place, like a museum piece.

A sense of something missing haunts the hall.
It throws a shadow, though it has no mass –
its presence real, its color black, its shape
rectangular, behind the trophy case,
where Father Geoghan's portrait used to hang.

Doré's Engravings

The leaves are dry and yellow, edged with brown,
in the Forest of the Suicides. One soul
bares his knothole-navel, while his neck
grows down, a tuberous root, into the hard
unholy ground:

       Mr. Potato Head,
my brother says. Following his lead,
I laugh with him, pretending to be brave
or pitiless, uncertain which is which.
(In Hell, the difference doesn't matter much.)

Harpies – with claws, human heads, crows' wings
and women's breasts – alight on limbs to eat
the leaves of trees that moan aloud and bleed;

feet protrude from smoking wells, intestines
dangle from a stomach wound, lopped limbs
fester perpetually for finite sins;

while bathed in love-light, angels tra-la-la
and beam as sinners scream. Then, at the end,
the wingèd creatures swarm in corkscrew form,

spiraling up to God. But Tommy says
they're swirling down the toilet; and, being ten,
he makes a farting noise, and says amen.

Lourdes

A trickle from a single spring
heals a few who travel to your grotto
high in the Pyrenees. You're hard to get to,
and can't fix everything.

One wound, one tumor at a time –
why must your miracles be watered down?
Let limbs regrow from stumps in Sierra Leone.
Now that would be a sign.

Burst the spigots. Overflow.
Send mercy surging down the mountainside,
washing over every borderline.
Don't just stand there. Go

to battlefields and seek us out.
Hurry, before the bodies start to smell.
Repack that soldier's brains inside his skull.
Cure my doubt.

Guadalupe

Spanish roses, dozens of them,
freshly picked in mid-December,
spill from Juan Diego's *tilma*.
Zumarraga stares in wonder.

Virgen Morena, Blessèd Mother,
Holy Queen, Tonantzin's daughter,
conqueror of Quetzalcoatl,
champion of the poor and humble,

wrap the stars around your shoulders,
make the sun your gold corona,
ride the moon, a blackened sliver
lifted high on eagle feathers.

Guadalupe, hear my prayer,
be you saint or Aztec goddess,
heal the earth, cast out the darkness.
Evil times are now upon us.

Zeitoun

Zeitoun, Cairo, 1968

What if you were, as I suspect,
a hologram,
a Coptic tourist trap, a scam
the mortal eye could not detect?

What if photons, fiddled with,
beguiled the eye,
glittering in the Cairo sky,
a brilliant flimflam veiled in myth?

What if the world, wanting a mother,
embraced a ruse,
thousands of Muslims, Christians, Jews,
fooled into seeing the light together?

And what if the only light to see
is in the faces
of foolish crowds in sacred places?
Our Lady of Light, enlighten me.

Parking Garage

Time was, she'd go for walks in yellow woods
alone, alert for deer, and certain trees
whose "souls" she liked pretending she could hear.

Now she prefers to stay indoors, reclined
in TV mode, or cubicled at work
when all the other worker-drones have gone.

Tonight, her heel-clicks echo in the empty
cavern of an underground garage
where light bores dark with its fluorescent hum,

and as she walks, and fumbles for her keys,
she notices the walls and concrete floors
are speaking in the tongues of certain trees.

Penal Rosary

By sleight of hand, he manages to twist
his ring from thumb to finger secretly.
Five fingers hide one cross inside a fist,
ten beads against a palm, one mystery:
his faith in what he feels but cannot see.

Decades pass. Now priests, now witches burn;
sinner and saint converge as tables turn
until Crusader's one with Saracen.
Our penance is to learn what to unlearn
and, having come full circle, start again.

Science

Neanderthal Bone Flute

"...if it really is a flute, it provides significant evidence that Neanderthals may have been the equal of Homo Sapiens in the evolution of humankind." – Wikipedia.com, "Divje Babe"

Let it be a flute. Let some young man,
perhaps red-haired, have carved it just for fun.
Or better yet, to serenade someone:
one of the jut-chinned girls, not of his clan,
a stranger from the east. And let his genes
thrive still in solitary types, the shy
who fidget when you look them in the eye,
the tongue-tied, who must woo by other means.

Ignore the new genetic tests that say
the girl rejected him, that winter came
and spear could not compete with bow and arrow;
that want, or slaughter, whittled him away
because his ways and ours were not the same.
Let bone be flute, the music in our marrow.

Impulse

By thinking – up, back, swivel to the right –
a Rhesus brain controls a robot's arm
over a wireless channel; while tonight
you keep me warm

under the covers with your fevered skin,
hairy as any ape. In either case
an impulse jumps a synapse; dreams begin
to take up space

in ways that bodies do. The high-pitched whine
of monkey-driven metal switching gears,
the interlocking of your legs with mine,
are just ideas

telegraphed into things: thoughts that stray
from gray matter to motor, leaving grooves
of memory that run whichever way
the spirit moves.

The First Uprising

The blackest plums are closest to the sun.
Eve, with a yen for something sweeter, stands
unsteadily, and with her furry hands
reaches up and plucks the ripest one.
Her brothers watch with envy till they learn
her trick of rearing up; then they compete,
tottering on their hind legs as they eat.
The youngest gnaws the tough green bulbs they spurn.

With height, enlightenment. Now they can see
above the brush, across the burning plains:
a herd, a stream, a wolf that might attack.
But God knows what their legacy will be:
the shifting pelvic bones, the labor pains,
the feeling that they've strayed and can't go back.

Hologram

This is a hologram of me
that fades and flickers as it stirs
the soup. Unseen machinery
projects my flesh; an engine whirs
behind the wall, and generates
repeating waves of sound and heat.
A pulsing pattern simulates
a skin devoid of blood or meat.

The hologram is sputtering
with static, and the color's dim,
but it continues buttering
his bread, and that's enough for him;
while you are unimpressed, who own
the best of me: the pulp, the bone.

Lovesick

Don't look away, you gave me this disease.
A carrier, you passed it unawares.
My every cell is altered now; each bears
your stamp, a mutant, every drop of me
adulterated. If I could, I'd squeeze
the stinging poison out. It's in my hair,
my fingernails, each microscopic pair
of spiral strands, corrupting by degrees.

Geneticists who study me on slides
could piece you back together. My remains
will carry traces, in these scalded veins,
of your warm hand; in my triglycerides,
and in the deepest etchings of my brain,
they'll find the you my body memorized.

Gingernut

Naked on auction blocks, pale eyes
blinking in the southern sun, they fetched
the most gold for looking least at home.
Their skin, woodland white, like Indian pipe,
demanded special protection; and for that
the Romans prized them all the more.

The Vikings gave it to the Irish:
fire from Iceland. Blood, from battle axes
long rusted into henna streaks in mud,
scours the plain, a blush invades –
red braids flying behind, spiked flail whirling –
thundering on horseback over throat and face.

Snow leopards carried down-mountain,
skittish in bamboo cages, are no more exotic,
the blacksmith's neon bloom no more electric,
moonshine, fire ants, volcanoes, cayenne candy,
pornography, scarlet fever, the burst of orange
that comes with a fist in the face, no more intense
than Rusty at crest and crotch; nor is the fox
with its slim black feet more elegantly dressed.

How Ticklishness Evolved

What danger does he shrink from, when my nail
skitters across the boundary of his tan –
a tiger's whisker-tip, a scorpion's tail?
What wriggler wrecked a cave bear's dinner plan
by waking up the world's first ticklish man?

Maybe it was a spider's needle feet
that triggered that first trembling retreat;
perhaps the flicking of a serpent's tongue,
or something more insidious and sweet,
whose touch was feather-soft before it stung.

Rays at Cape Hatteras

The cownose rays are showing off today.
They flip themselves like flapjacks over pans
of Carolina surf, and when one lands,
the splat reverberates a mile away.
Sometimes you see the backs of their whale-gray
pectoral fins, outstretched like flipper-hands;
or else they show their bellies as they dance,
white slabs with grins carved out, as if from clay.

In great outlays of energy, they burst
through breakers, moved by some instinctive wish
to flounder in the air. Their flight is brief
and clumsy, evolution having cursed
these would-be herons with the flesh of fish:
rude fliers in the face of disbelief.

People

The Hybrid

He's still got hooves in back;
there's still a market for those pickled feet.
The market decides what's poison and what's meat.
The market is why he's got no twisty tail,
no swinging sack.

But you can tell he's male;
we left that there so he can urinate.
(He's even toilet-trained!) No need to mate.
We clone them, so instead of sows, there's just
a paper trail.

Those peons eat his dust;
look at him work. We gave him human hands,
and brains enough so that he understands
how to assemble circuit boards. He works
because he must;

devoid of human quirks,
he thinks of working, and of working only.
He's never restless, angry, sad, or lonely.
We're hoping soon to breed a whole new line
of super-clerks,

then, educated swine:
economists, or even presidents.
The market will decide if that makes sense.
And when they're plump enough, they'll taste divine
with the right wine.

Famine Ship

Sweet was the smell that wafted from the hold
six weeks ago, when we were hauling rum
and sugar from Havana: goods we sold
for twice their worth in Dublin. Now we come
bearing cargo no one wants to buy,
these rank paupers headed for Quebec.
When fever hits, the old are first to die.
We bury them at sea, then swab the deck.

"...the house of the Lord forever." Sunlight streams
down on the lightweight corpse. It almost seems
that God is smiling on us from above.
But then that cursèd wailing from below,
where scores are burning up, reminds me of
the freight we carried twenty years ago.

Not Our Dog

We tried for years, haphazardly at first,
and then got serious; we bought some books,
journals with checkboxes, thermometers
and little strips I stained with minus signs.
Technology was offered; we declined.

Plan B is now Plan A, and none too soon.
I've got paint swatches for the middle room,
various things to whitewash, or scrub clean,
no time for news. The Globe sits rolled, unread.

But trouble spies on us behind the blinds,
a giant dog that's caught our scent. At night,
its eyewhite glows between the slats, its breath
fogs the windowpane; and while we hide
at home, the mangy world of war, disease
and famine hunkers down to wait for us.

One day my future daughter will ask why
her arms are so much tawnier than mine.
I'll answer, you were chosen, your first mother
nobly gave her baby up; but how
does one defend the boundaries of love –
"Too bad about your mum, but life is tough"?

Outside, the cold and darkness settle in
on snug suburban rooftops; and the dog
growls low in its throat, and bares its teeth at me
while I choose curtains for the nursery.

Business Trip

The demo had gone well.
Still talking shop, we walked to our hotel
through thinning crowds, down the uneven street,
sweltering in Beijing's mid-August heat
as evening fell.

Tomorrow we'd be gone,
these bustling people, these bewildering signs
a dreamscape disappearing with the dawn.
We'd live in English, stab our food with tines,
forget, move on.

A woman, small and thin,
tapped me and said something in Mandarin
I couldn't understand. A sleeping child
lay draped across her chest. I stammered, smiled,
expressed chagrin,

then feeling left behind
hurried away to catch up with the rest,
failing an unexpected litmus test.
We stopped for cocktails, eager to unwind
with our own kind.

The Petition

Somerville, MA, ca. 1909

They came at night, but didn't burn a cross,
those well-bred Northerners. Instead they stood
looking apologetic on the porch.
Their leader held a lantern, not a torch.

"*Mi scusi,* speak the English not so good,"
Maria Rosa smiled, confused. But then
they read it to her slowly. Rearing up,
she shook her fist and shouted at the men,

"Leave us alone, or I sell the house to nigger!"
It worked. They all turned whiter than they were
and never tried to mess with her again.

Or so my father says. Ashamed of her,
we tell the story with a guilty snigger,
pretending to be shocked. But at the bone
we know the secret gospel. Life's a cup;
each sip you take is someone else's loss.
Boo hoo. Salut. You take care of your own.

Laissez-Faire

"[The overpopulation of Ireland] being altogether beyond the power of man, the cure has been applied by the direct stroke of an all-wise Providence..." – Charles Trevelyan, British Treasury Secretary, 1846

The extra folk. The fat. The gristle.
Ragweed, nettle, buckthorn, thistle.
Girls in shirtwaist factories.
Brushwood burned to free the trees.
Dusty little Mom-and-Pops.
Apple peelings, turnip tops.
The latchkey kid, the lemon rind,
the poor New Orleans left behind.
The trampled ant, the straying sheep,
the badly schooled, the compost heap
that must decay to feed the crop.
John Henry's carcass, should he drop;
his life, his living, should he live.
The damn we frankly do not give.
The sack in which we drown the whelp
(as Nature sometimes needs our help).

War of the Worlds

Driving to work that morning, I was struck
by something funny on the radio:
a prankster claimed two planes had run amok
and shut Manhattan down. Perhaps this show
paid homage to that hoax by Orson Welles
in '38. The newsmen played it straight –
impressive parody! Such bagatelles
so often carry unintended weight.

The novelty worn off, I turned the knob
to hear the same report on other stations.
Arriving stunned at work, I did my job,
seeing no point in tears or lamentations;
preferring to go on just as before
but loving what I loved a little more.

An Old Song

Will he come home in the morning, morning,
    Home with the rising sun,
With a "Sorry I'm late" and a "Kiss me Kate"
    And a sweet for the youngest one?

Will he come home a-whistling, whistling,
    Over the hill and down,
With a wink and a whirl for his only girl,
    And me in my dressing gown?

Could he be now a-striding, striding,
    Over the crimson field,
And his knitted bones be strong as stones,
    And his every wound be healed?

Could he be now a-rising, rising,
    Gathering up his soul,
And his muddy bed no more be red,
    And his limbs be strong and whole?

Will he come home in the morning, morning,
    Shouldering high his gun,
With a squeak o' the gate and a "Kiss me Kate"
    After the war is done?

Perversity

Ditty

The saddest songs are those that drip
like sweat down the sides of a lemonade pitcher.
Sing me a drink about money gone missing,
serve it up tart with a hillbilly twist:
the bitterer the better, to make the mouth pucker
and gather up the slack.

The saddest songs are those that burn
black as a match and a bundle o' tinder.
Kindle a ditty on daddy gone drifting,
wind it around with a pennywhistle riff;
slowly unroll each note, dark
as smoke from a chimney stack.

The saddest songs are those that fade
like footprints over Siberian tundra.
Shiver the strings of a welcome winter,
shovel it under, drumbeat deep;
naked and bleak as the trees of Tunguska,
laid out back to back.

Lye

In Massachusetts, air itself
is made of lye;
its wire brushes scrub the front
but spare the lee.

It scours the granite stones that line
the island beach,
corrodes the shells of horseshoe crabs,
blisters the birch.

Displaced, I miss the shabbiness
of cedar shingles
bleeding out, from red to gray
at shoreward angles,

rust that roughens up the steel
of warehouse walls,
the shipyard's reddened gray, the scab
that never heals.

Shotgun

His smoke shoots down her throat, an urgent stream
she likes the more because of where it's been.
He's giving it to her. She takes it in.
It's not the weed that makes her green eyes gleam,
but pride. Ha! If only Mary Ann
could see her now! Those skinny twelve-year-old
St. Paulsies with their clammy hands can't hold
a candle to this dreamy, mustached man.

He whispers, "God, I shouldn't be doing this."
Forbidden! Secret! Sin! The trinity
of yumminess. A woman of mystery,
she's snaring him with her seductive wiles.
"Aw, don't be such a wuss." They quasi-kiss
again. His lashes lower: two black smiles.

Brockton Man

In newsprint gray, a friendly face
greets me from the Local section:
bearded, young, with just a trace
of resignation

tugging at one brow, the eyes
meeting mine – but no, not quite,
they're fixed on something just beyond,
at earring height.

He's cut his hair, I see. Looks good.
And from a glimpse of neck I know
the rest: the veiny arms he had
ten years ago

still white-hot, rivered with blue,
the tender skin, still prone to burn.
A headline calls the youth I knew
Brockton Man,

as if he were some ancient skull,
perhaps not human, scientists
dug up. But modern man can kill
with his bare fists,

and knives are only sharpened stones.
Excuses, too, are nature's law.
He stabbed her more than twenty times;
her children saw;

but that was the drugs, my heart contends,
and if I feel a twinge of lust
remembering those tapered bands
of muscle, just

or unjust doesn't enter in,
nor grief for someone I don't miss
and never having known, can't mourn.
Only this,

of all instincts, best and worst:
to bond, to bend, to waive, to waver,
to put unruly feelings first,
and gloss it over.

At Sea

Mermaid

The captain fears she'll try to drag them under,
luring them with her song, her nakedness,
and tells the other men to stop their ears.
Her calls to them are met with hoots and jeers.

They turn away before she starts to founder,
trying to swim but sinkered by her dress
which, with its petticoats, can't help but slow
the frantic scissor-kicking just below.

Small town. The ninth-grade girl who ran away
returns with the smell of monster on her skin,
more a secretion than a residue.
Her father gave a reading yesterday
in church. How mortified he must have been.
Disgraceful, what she put her parents through.

Pirate

He didn't know they suffered for their spoils,
scanning the same horizon every day;
whole weeks becalmed, floating in stagnant scum,
living on weeviled bread and watered rum.

He didn't expect the smelly, swabby toils,
the constant threat of scurvy, lice, lost pay,
night after rough, disoriented night
trapped in the open, with no land in sight.

At Sea

His stomach rumbles as he walks the floor,
scanning the Greyhound crowd for older men
who never board their buses. Broke again
and bored, he loiters near the open door,
watching as a cyclist fishtails through
the traffic on Atlantic Avenue.

Hermit Crab

She feels at home in this hard place, each whorl
familiar, somehow, in advance. Inside
she's soft – but hiding in a borrowed hide
changes the animal. Some creatures curl
around a columella naturally,
as if the shell were part of them. They're true
and false to their anatomy; they do
and don't become what they pretend to be.

Pup

Born fully formed, a shark in miniature,
he quickly catches on. Unlike the others
 – baby whales dependent on their mothers,
or tadpoles, larvae, soft and immature –
he's instantly at ease in his own gunmetal
gray, unyielding skin. The youngster feeds
himself, and someday, if he's lucky, breeds;
his chances of survival slim to none.

At Sea

Wrack

Kept afloat by tiny balloons, unanchored
seaweed bobs and drifts with the waves in masses.
Named for grapes in Portuguese, limp sargassum
stinks like a drunkard,
sloshes like the hair of a sodden woman
washing up unwanted the morning after.
Every turning tide, there's another dozen
drowned in salt water.

Breakers

Reason gives way to the sound of the surf,
    the repetitive pounding,
pounding of waves as they break, the vicarious
    pleasure of breaking,
slamming the sand, stunning and stunned.
    There's a natural reason
some of us love their oblivious rhythm –
    unreasoning, mind you;
mindless as in not minding, a rubbery
    hide like a porpoise,
blissfully, blissfully empty of purpose.
    Empty of empathy,
boys in the lot compete for the fun of it,
    aiming their empties
carefully, shutting one eye, so they break
    at the feet of a wino;
laughing and laughing as bottles explode
    into glittering sea spray
under a streetlight.

Sea Monster

Cold doesn't sneak in like a parasite
and multiply, it's something you become:
a single-minded organism, numb
and numbskulled, chattering alingually.
What a wiggly two-headed trilobite
we made with all our arms and legs that night
in someone's foyer; dragged up from the sea,
bedraggled, at the end of our one rope.
Wrapped in a single coat, we shared a skin,
a bottle, a kiss, blue-lipped and Cambrian,
our tiny brain too primitive to cope
with any concept so Darwinian
as hope; just body heat and you and me.
Dumb animal, and near-extinct, but then
there are worse things to be.

Oyster

A bit of grit.
She treasures it.

Old School

I see him now: the old-school formalist
moored in a leather wing chair in his study,
half-lenses lowered. "Young lady, I insist
on perfect rhyme..." A handsome fuddy-duddy
who puffs a pipe and writes like Thomas Hardy,
he grades me with a grim parade of X's,
doubling my demerits when I'm tardy.
His strictures are as sure as death and taxes.

I see him then: his Latin master flexes
the cane before him as he conjugates.
He trembles, then remembers, and relaxes;
relieved, recites, and sits. Today he breaks
the rules but rarely, taking pleasure in
the piquant joys of English discipline.

The Poet Who Will Win This Competition

studied Latin and Greek, and lets us know.
Doesn't need to Google "Philoctetes."
Was born approximately thirty years ago.

In high school, did her homework. Ate her Wheaties.
Strove, as an only child, to please her mom.
Dated a jock. Resisted his entreaties

until the time was right: her senior prom.
(Was able to go; her boyfriend wasn't thirty.)
Never played Russian roulette, or built a bomb

from cigarettes and butane. Wasn't nerdy,
just clever. Never ran away from home.
Never got paid for doing something dirty,

or snapped her gum, or stole a pocket comb.
Thinks poets who write of lurid things are lame
sensationalists; that life's the Hippodrome,

that she's in front, though others, to their shame,
take shortcuts. Never snorted something blue,
got lost in the amusement park, and came

home with a rash from only God knows who.
Never wrote anything foolish. Takes her fame
in stride; expects it. Never says "fuck you."

Poor Dolores

Dolores wears her melancholy well.
It drapes in languid folds along the lines
of her long thighs, a satin black expanse,
an extravagant expense of sulks and sighs.
Each tear becomes a diamond as it dries.

Each man who meets her longs to lie beneath
the weeping willows of her hair, and hopes
to glimpse the woodland nymph that crouches there.
Shadows tremble in her collarbones
like shallow cups of sorrow, sweet and rare.

> Other women weep and no one cares;
> their ugly snuffles only irritate.
> When funerals and tumors slow them down
> their bosses yell at them for being late.
> They stand in stalls and flush to hide their cries.

Dolores, though, is differently configured.
Around her hanging head, white butterflies
flutter in a sympathetic halo.
Of all the maids that mourn with heaving breast,
poor, poor Dolores does it best.

Gulp

Did Eve,
I wonder, have
a thing
for throats:
the sweep of cord
to clavicle,
the deepening
of muscle-grooves
with strain;

the way a blade
makes it swallow
hard; one's point,
though gently made,
not pressed,
made plain;

the little hollow
at its base, where
collarbones,
awkward as a pair
of gawky teens,
have left a kiss-
sized space;

there, where
the handsome
highwayman
wore lace;

and there,
midway between
anonymous man

and mien,
the tender swell,
the drag queen's
one
inevitable tell,
bobbing like
a bell above
a chapel;

did Eve,
I wonder, love
the vulnerable
curve
of Adam's
apple?

Noted Sadomasochists

Jean-Jacques Rousseau

Impossible, unnatural; a knight
can't ask for that. No blushing heroine
could love a stooping, groveling Gawain.
Mon Dieu! She'd shriek with laughter at the sight,

summoning all her maids, who'd point and taunt,
and tell the world your secret. In her eyes
you'd be grotesque, a clown with a disease.
Some things it's just ridiculous to want.

To go on wanting hurts a little less
at any given moment, a slow flame
under the spit you'll die on, in due time.
So hush. It would be madness to confess.

Algernon Swinburne

In the heart of Hermaphroditus,
    Where the hawk is at one with the dove,
Contradictions that shock and delight us
    Are joined in a curious love.
In the virtuous mouth of a devil,
    A curse and a kiss are the same,
So an innocent sinner may revel
    In glorious shame.

In the brilliance of gold that is beaten,
    In the wrath of a merciful god,
In the noble traditions of Eton,
    In the serpent that rose from the rod,

Noted Sadomasochists

May be found a contrarian beauty
    That appeals to poetical men
Who respond to its call, as to duty,
    Again and again.

Percy Grainger

Some folks are strangely strung,
tuned to the low note's snap and quiver,
fond of songs with a sharper flavor,
licks that burn the tongue.

They love the echoing
of conga drums and booming basses,
shivering skins that hardwood kisses,
rhythm in full swing.

Each beat's a heartfelt thing.
The cymbal as it sways and hisses,
wailing sax and bellowing brasses,
summon up some pang

experienced when young,
some chord too often struck, forever
played in the bloodstream, over and over,
wordless but well sung.

Lawrence of Arabia

I know a guilty tribe condemned to roam
forever in the Wilderness of Zin,

not Jews, not Bedouin,
not free to leave and never quite at home.

No savior makes them pay for what they've done.
They live to starve, and only eat what's bitter;
they love to drink hard water
and labor in the brutal desert sun.

Their crime's forgotten now. That hardly matters
to sinners of their stripe, who pay and pay
and still can't walk away,
preferring to remain eternal debtors.

C. S. Lewis

God, for our own good, is sometimes cruel,
letting blood from the sacrificial lamb,
whether on the front lines at the Somme
or an English school.

His love is fearsome, irresistible:
a love that draws us to its cleansing flame
against our will, until our souls succumb
to its urgent pull.

He is the master, we the little boy
who, kicking and screaming, learns at last to find,
in lessons he has yet to understand,
surprising joy.

Kink

The others stand upright, but not this pine
that thrusts its swayback out over the pond
clawing at noon's face. It started straight,
but here, waist high, it curls around a space
once filled by something bigger than itself.
A sapling then, it grew up in the shade
between a rock, most likely, and a hard place.
Or maybe it was buffeted by winds –
punishing downdrafts from the north, its stock
still immature – and couldn't stand its ground.
Who knows? Could have been something in the seed
itself, telling it to twist, and crouch, and sniff
at dirty life, unsmitten with the sky;
a skin of algae sometimes broken by
a blacksnake's graceful writhings – harmless things –
and snapping turtles who sunbathe on its limbs.

Rootbound

Every cell still tells it to dig in the dirt
as far as roots can reach; to make it rain
upside down, to fly in earth, to stretch
down, away from the sun, finding the route
to heaven through a harder, darker sky.

Love

Random Sextet

1

He came back from the army with no hair,
a razor job, and that's what got me thinking
how ugly he was: all bones and freckles where
his chestnut bangs had been. We went out drinking
and I broke up with him; his tearful pleas
embarrassed me. They shipped him overseas.

2

My older brother had him over. "Seize
the day," I figured, letting down my hair,
then spent the next four years trying to please
that callous motherfucker. What was I thinking?
He only wanted me when he'd been drinking.
But he knew what to do, and how, and where.

3

He did the lambada, wholly unaware
how silly he looked. He'd come from overseas,
Hungarian, I think: "Let me keep dreenking
in the sight of you, your leeps, your hair..."
I sang his praises, loudly, later, thinking,
"He's corny, but at least he aims to please."

4

His eyes were blue, his face designed to please
the eye, an Irishman. I'd make him wear
blue shirts. But as I kissed him, I'd be thinking
about his poor fiancee overseas.
And so I'd cry, and muss his rusty hair;
then both of us would laugh and keep on drinking.

5

He picked me up one night when I'd been drinking
(he was a cabbie). Gagging, I said, "Please
pull over"; he obliged, and held my hair.
That weekend he wore Tarzan underwear.
But college had me frantic over Cs,
and he preferred me when I wasn't thinking.

6

He'd robbed a bank and gone to prison, thinking
he'd find his stash and spend all summer drinking
once he got out. But the god who oversees
the fates of losers foiled him. "Honey, please,
I'll pay you back tomorrow." Everywhere
he went, he spent. But he had awesome hair.

The Pig and the Pearl

See how it pains him, wedged inside the cleft
of his hind hoof? He's limping, ma'am. He's hurt,
that's why he hops, and shuffles to the left,
trying to shake it free. A clump of dirt,
a pebble, some dried dung, it's all the same –

You shake your head, you smile, but truly, ma'am,
I wouldn't pull your leg.
                            Oh, sure, he's tame,
but still, he's just a hog. A honey ham.

Beg pardon?
               No, of course he doesn't bite –
your pig's a gentle creature, I admit –
but even so, what makes you think he might
have any use for *that*? He rolls in shit!

Ma'am, with all due respect, my word upon it:
take back your precious gift. He doesn't want it.

Scrape

Silly enough being forty and not having read the *Aeneid*;
sillier still, to get carried away at the orthopedist's,
squished between fidgety, purse-obsessed women while overhead,
    Oprah
lectures the audience, goddess of talk, demanding attention.

Still, there's no telling the throat not to strangle itself, or the gut to
stop contracting. Reason's no match for the body – not when
Dido's heart is bashing itself on the bars of your rib cage.

God, how embarrassing! Best you can do is to flee to the restroom,
knowing they'll call you the moment you leave. You'll miss your
    appointment
blubbering over a fictional character. What is your *problem*?
Happily married, too! But Aeneas, Aeneas is leaving,
turning his back on her, boarding his ship, setting sail, disappearing.
Neck pain forgotten now, all you can feel is the scrape of an old
blade on your breastbone.

Made in Minnesota

It would have been a winter day when they
produced the movie forty years ago:
wolves elude the lens, refuse to play
for unmanned cameras hidden in the snow;

and drawling Nordic men with eyes that droop
withdraw behind their newspapers to puff
on pipes, while big-boned, silent women stoop
to lift their loads alone. Their hands are rough.

And I can see you as a baby there,
weaned abruptly, and too early, from
the breast your mother didn't like to bare,
the house being drafty, and her fingers numb.

Irises

He sees only the rhizomes
rustling like onions in corrugated cardboard,
withered bodies packed and shipped for burial;
not the blooms,

not the tentacles that poke and feel around
underground, searching for new home turf,
not the shoots breaking virgin earth.

Even in June, when tight throats open,
exhaling shades of sherbet and hot violet,
he sees only the petals,
not the pistils.

Mortimer

The dummy never sleeps. His body lies
inside a suitcase that his master locks,
and all night long he stares through lidless eyes.
His heart is buried in a cedar box.
It, too, is wood, consisting of some hidden
knobs and levers on a swivel-stick
he can't control. Words rise from him, unbidden;
his humor hinges on a magic trick.

Behind the boyish frame, a veteran voice
co-opts him as a witness on the stand
who's made to cover up – he has no choice –
the thrustings of an uninvited hand.
And yet, alone, he thinks with longing of
those furtive fingers, all he knows of love.

Love Sonnet

The soldierness of your astronomy
so gentle hungries in my panging blue,
it shivers the metal mail, unrusting you,
unresting in the owlest leaves of me.

Pitier velvets, trembler sheets of glass,
more forest bloods, of piner hills bereft,
never endeared a dawn; nor fawned a theft
with sharper slenders from more willing grass.

O fain would I elfing go, and bladeful sleep
amid the winter-bell's unthroated soft,
never to sweet again your ladly cry,

if bellward be your summer's lively-keep;
and wolfen salt that cheeks your lash aloft
were petal-dreamt upon the elfer's eye.

Flipside

For joy like this, the only words I know
I've had to borrow from the other side:
knocked out, steamrollered, damn, I almost died,
familiar phrases for some crushing blow
that brings you to your knees. I've been laid low
by love, ground into dust by heaven's wheels.
Funny how much like this rock bottom feels,
the tears, the weakness, and the letting go.

My blessing: may you, in your turn, break down
and lose your marbles. May you fall apart,
be smashed to smithereens and blown away,
scattered in all directions. May you drown.
May happiness make mincemeat of your heart,
and helpless, may you wring your hands and pray.

What She Sees in Him

both the proposal
and the pose

the alabaster
and the rose

the craggy shell
the mother-of-pearl

the stubble cheek
the stubborn curl

horse and harness
ox and yoke

strength that trembles
at each stroke

the iron chain
its weakest link

both the armor
and the chink

To My Husband, Poetry,

apparently, does not have callused hands.
It went to college, has a smart C. V.,
and knows the reason for the leftmost fork.
It doesn't wear a uniform to work.

Still, he endures this reading for my sake
unmoved, unnoticed as a wall. At home
where nouns defer to what they name, he'd pluck
a pencil from behind his ear and mark

the meeting-points of bookshelf and support;
or putter in silence, putting up storm doors
I'd never have remembered to install.
He's too concrete for words. A concrete wall

is constant, rough enough to face the sand.
Noise, weakness and worry break against it
like water on the Hull seawall in winter
when stilted houses shiver on dry land.

Notes

Gingernut: "Gingernut" is a slang term for a person with red or ginger hair. According to several dubious Internet sources, fair-skinned redheads often fetched the highest prices in Roman slave markets.

Noted Sadomasochists: C. S. Lewis once said he came to Christianity "kicking and screaming." His autobiography is *Surprised By Joy*. As an archaeologist, T. E. Lawrence (Lawrence of Arabia) co-wrote a report titled "The Wilderness of Zin."

Penal Rosary: The penal rosary was a single-decade rosary used during the Penal Times in Ireland. It was easily concealed in the hand. An attached ring was moved from finger to finger as each decade was prayed.

Zeitoun: An image of the Virgin Mary appeared repeatedly over the Coptic Orthodox Church of Saint Demiana in Zeitoun, Cairo between 1968 and 1971. The apparition, which was seen by people of various faiths and nationalities, is sometimes referred to as Our Lady of Light.

Index of Titles and First Lines

A Note About the Author

Rose Kelleher was born in 1964, grew up in Massachusetts and earned her B.A. in English at UMass Boston. She has worked as a technical writer and programmer, and authored four computer books and numerous technical articles. Since rediscovering poetry in recent years, she has published poems and essays in a variety of magazines – including *Anon, Atlanta Review,* the *Dark Horse, First Things, iota, Measure,* the *Shit Creek Review, Snakeskin* and *Verse Daily* – and been nominated twice for the Pushcart Prize. She lives with her husband in Gaithersburg, Maryland. For more information, please visit her website at www.ramblingrose.com.

Other books from Waywiser

*Expanded UK edition